Animal Eggs

written by Jay Dale

This mother bird
is sitting on her eggs.
The eggs are in a nest.

Look!

Here comes a baby bird.

The baby bird

is coming out of the egg.

Look!

Here come the baby crocodiles.

Baby crocodiles

come out of eggs, too!

Can you see the mother ostrich?
She is sitting on her eggs.
A mother ostrich will sit
on her eggs all day.

A father ostrich
will sit
on the eggs, too.

Look!

An ostrich egg is **very** big.

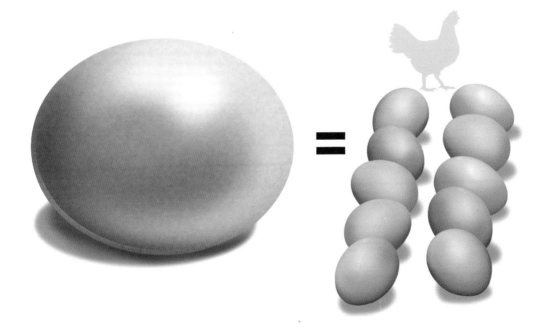

Can you see the baby ostrich?
The baby ostrich
is coming out of the big egg.

Here is a mother turtle.
She is in the sand.

Look at all her eggs.

Baby turtles come out of eggs, too.

Look!
The baby turtles
are out of the eggs.

Can you see the baby animals?
They are coming out of the eggs.